Schriftenreihe des Stadtarchivs Heidelberg
Sonderveröffentlichung 17

Im Auftrag
der Stadt Heidelberg herausgegeben
von Peter Blum

Heidelberg Once and Today

Comparative Sights of the City

David Depenau
Ernot Drücke

Heidelberg einst und heute

Vergleichende Stadtansichten

2008
Edition Guderjahn
verlag regionalkultur

Für Jasper, Julia, Katharina, Mattis und Neele

Titelbilder: Blick auf den Marstall von Norden im Jahr 1896 (oben) und 2008 (unten)

Bibliographische Information der Deutschen Bibliothek
Die Deutsche Bibliothek verzeichnet diese Publikation in der Deutschen Nationalbibliographie; detaillierte bibliographische Daten sind im Internet über http://dnb.ddb.de abrufbar.

Schriftenreihe des Stadtarchivs Heidelberg, Sonderveröffentlichung 17

Herausgeber	Dr. Peter Blum, im Auftrag der Stadt Heidelberg
Autoren	David Depenau (Text & Konzept), Ernot Drücke (Fotos), Dr. Mirko Wittwar (Translation)
Titel	Heidelberg einst und heute
Untertitel	Vergleichende Stadtansichten

Herstellung	verlag regionalkultur (vr)
Redaktion und Satz	Harald Funke (vr)
Endkorrektur	Eberhard Guderjahn, Heidelberg
Umschlaggestaltung	Jochen Baumgärtner (vr)

ISBN 978-3-89735-544-6

Diese Publikation ist auf alterungsbeständigem und säurefreiem Papier (TCF nach ISO 9706) gedruckt entsprechend den Frankfurter Forderungen.

verlag regionalkultur
Heidelberg – Ubstadt-Weiher – Neustadt a.d.W. – Basel

Korrespondenzadresse:
Bahnhofstraße 2 • 76698 Ubstadt-Weiher • Telefon (07251) 36703-0 • Fax 36703-29
eMail: kontakt@verlag-regionalkultur.de • Internet: www.verlag-regionalkultur.de

Geleitwort

Städte verändern sich. Nicht immer sind Kriege dafür verantwortlich. Oft sind es eher lokal begrenzte, ja schleichende Veränderungen, indem Bestehendes entsprechend den sich wandelnden Anforderungen menschlichen Lebens modernisiert wird. Im Nachhinein erweist sich vielfach erst und bei genauerer Betrachtung, dass nicht jede Anpassung an die Zeitumstände der Lebensqualität zugute kam. Mitunter ist das Gegenteil der Fall.

Die Gegenüberstellung historischer und aktueller Fotos ist in mehrfacher Hinsicht reizvoll. Sie dokumentiert, dass Heidelberg eine schöne, lebens- wie liebenswerte Stadt ist, die in den letzten Jahrhunderten von Kriegen, aber auch von Bausünden weitgehend verschont geblieben ist. Vieles erscheint vertraut. Mitunter aber bieten sich unerwartete wie überraschende Einblicke. Der kritische Blick auf die heutige Situation am südlichen Neckarufer im Umfeld von Marstall und Stadthalle und der unmittelbare Vergleich mit früher mag freilich auch andeuten, dass und wo sich Lebensqualität zurückgewinnen lässt. Denn der Blick zurück eröffnet im Einzelfall bisweilen ungewohnte Perspektiven, zeigt z.B. auf Höhe des alten Schlachthofes Freiflächen und einen unbehinderten Zugang zum Neckarufer; beides ist seit der Errichtung des Neckarstadens verloren gegangen. So bietet die vorliegende Schrift einen in vielfältiger Weise anregenden Vergleich mit dem einst und jetzt.

Dr. Eckart Würzner
Oberbürgermeister

Preface

Cities change. Not always this is due to war. Often it is locally restricted, even creeping change, because that what exists is modernized according to changing demands of human life. In retrospect, in many cases and only at a closer look it becomes obvious that not every adjustment to the modes of time were in favour of the quality of life. Sometimes just the opposite is true.

Contrasting historic photographies to current ones is delightful in several respects. It documents that Heidelberg is a beautiful city, both worth to be loved and to live in, which in the course of the past centuries has ecaped wars but also buildings which might be a blot on the landscape. Many things look familiar. Sometimes, however, the observer is presented with both unexpected and surprising views. However, a critical look at today´s situation on the southern banks of the Neckar in the environment of "Marstall" and "Stadthalle" and the immediate comparison to the past may also give an idea of how quality of life might be regained. For in the individual case a look at the past offers unusual views, e. g. near the old slaughterhouse it discloses free space and an unhindered way to the Neckar, both of which has been lost since the erection of the "Neckarstaden". Thus, the here presented work offers a comparison of once and now which is stimulating in several respects.

Vorwort des Herausgebers

Bildbände über Heidelberg gab und gibt es viele. Mit unterschiedlichen Akzentuierungen. Mal mit historischem – mal mit mehr oder minder aktuellem Bildmaterial. Und bisweilen finden sich auch einige sehr ansprechende und interessante Bildbände darunter. Meist wird darin das frühere Heidelberg präsentiert. Und die Fotos besitzen oft einen ganz spezifischen Reiz, atmen die Atmosphäre einer vergangenen Zeit. Darüber hinaus sind sie eine wichtige Quelle, nicht allein wie Heidelberg früher aussah, sondern wie die Menschen hier wohnten, arbeiteten und lebten ...
Der vorliegende Bildband zeigt über den früheren Zustand hinaus, ob und was sich im unmittelbaren Vergleich zu heute verändert hat. Damit schlägt er den Bogen von der Vergangenheit zur Gegenwart. Und an manchen Orten scheint die Zeit tatsächlich schier stehen geblieben zu sein ... – Aber dieser Eindruck mag auch in der Vorgehensweise begründet liegen, die vom historischen Foto ausgehend nach dem Standort des damaligen Photographen fragte und ob heute von nahezu identischer Stelle aus eine Wiederholung der Aufnahme möglich ist. Auch der umgekehrte Weg erscheint lohnend. Das bleibt – vorerst noch – zukünftigen Veröffentlichungen vorbehalten, es sei aber bereits hier zur Anregung vermerkt.

Preface by the Editor

There have been many books of pictures on Heidelberg, and still there are many – with different emphases. Sometimes they offer historic pictures, and sometimes more or less current ones. And sometimes there are even some very appealing and interesting books of pictures among them. In most cases they present old Heidelberg. And often these photographies have their own, quite specific charme, they are full of the atmosphere of past times. Furthermore, they are an important historic source, not only in respect of what Heidelberg looked like in the past but of how people here were living, working, and how they were accomodated ...
Beyond presenting the situation of the past and by direct comparison, the here presented book of pictures shows if things have changed and if yes, in which ways. Thus the past is connected to the present. And indeed, at some places time really seems to be standing still ... – But this impression may also be due to the way of proceeding which, while starting out from the historic photography, asked about the location of the photographer in those days and if this photography might be repeated today from the almost identical place. Also doing it the other way round seems to be promising. But – at least for the time being – this must be left to future publications, it may only be remarked already here as an idea.

Dr. Peter Blum
Stadtarchivdirektor

Einleitung

Ein Spaziergang durch das Heidelberg des ausgehenden 19. Jahrhunderts? Viele mögen sich einen solchen Ausflug schon einmal gewünscht haben, ihn gar vor dem inneren Auge ausgeführt haben. Aber die nordbadische Universitätsstadt hat im letzten Jahrhundert Veränderungen erfahren, die einen solchen Rundgang heute bisweilen erschweren. Bei der Betrachtung von manchen Fotos aus jenen Tagen fällt es dem Leser mitunter schwer, sich die heutige Perspektive vorstellen zu können. Einerseits liegen Änderungen des Stadtbilds in der Natur der Sache: ohne Wachstum und Anpassung an geänderte Bedürfnisse wäre eine Stadt langfristig nicht (über-)lebensfähig. Andererseits hat nicht allein das natürliche Wachstum Heidelberg verändert. Wenn auch weniger die beiden Weltkriege, so haben doch Zeiten wenig sensiblen Vergangenheitsbewusstseins weitere Spuren im Gesicht der Stadt hinterlassen.
Die Autoren dieses Bildbandes haben es sich zur Aufgabe gemacht, die Aufmerksamkeit des Betrachters auf die mehr und weniger augenfälligen Veränderungen im Stadtbild Heidelbergs zu lenken.
Beim Betrachten der Fotos, die aus möglichst identischer Perspektive aufgenommen wurden, erkennt man Veränderungen, nicht immer nur zum Vorteil der jeweiligen Situation.
Die Autoren möchten die Leser zu einem Spaziergang durch Heidelberg einladen, der nicht auf der letzten Seite dieses Buches enden soll. Nehmen Sie das Buch als Vorlage und gehen Sie mit eigenen Augen auf eine interessante Entdeckungsreise durch die schöne historische Universitätsstadt Heidelberg.

David Depenau & Ernot Drücke

Introduction

A walk through Heidelberg at the end of the 19th century? Many may have wished to do such a trip, may even have been doing it in their minds. But in the course of the past century this university city in North Baden has experienced changes which today will sometimes make such a tour difficult. When looking at some photographies from those days, sometimes the reader finds it difficult to imagine today´s perspective. On the one hand, changes of the city´s view are quite natural: without growth and adjustment to changed demands, a city would not be able to survive on the long run. On the other hand, Heidelberg whas not only been changed by natural growth. If it was less the two world wars, indeed times of lacking consciousness of the past have left their marks on the view of the city.
The authors of this book of pictures made it their task to attract the observer´s attention to the more or less obvious changes of Heidelberg´s view.
When looking at photographies which were taken from the same angle, if ever possible, one will recognize changes, not always to the advantage of the respective situation.
The authors would like to invite the reader to a walk through Heidelberg which is not supposed to end at the last pages of this book. Take the book as a stimulation and use your own eyes for an interesting expedition through the beautiful, historic university city of Heidelberg.

Unterschiedliche Baustile vereint das Heidelberger Schloss, hier in einer Ansicht um 1890. Seine Bauzeit erstreckte sich über einige Jahrhunderte. Nach den Zerstörungen des 30jährigen Kriegs und Pfälzischen Erbfolgekriegs unterblieb ein Wiederaufbau. So hat sich eine Ruine erhalten, eine der schönsten der Welt.
Oberhalb des Schlosses, an Stelle der ehemaligen Oberen Burg, ist die nach 1851 erbaute Molkenkuranstalt zu erkennen. Der frühere Ziegenmilchausschank ist heute – vom gewachsenen Baumbestand fast verdeckt – das Restaurant zur Molkenkur. Das Schloss, nach wie vor eine der ersten touristischen Attraktionen Deutschlands, stellt sich dem Betrachter unverändert dar. Die Kanalisierung des Neckars in den 1920er Jahren dagegen hat den Neckar in ein begradigtes Bett gezwungen.

Heidelberger Schloss von Norden aus gesehen

The Heidelberger Schloss combines different building styles, here it is presented by a view from at about 1890. The entire building period stretched over some centuries. After destructions during the Thirty Years War and the War of the Palatinate Succession there was no reconstruction. Thus a ruin has been preserved, one of the most beautiful in the world.

Above the castle, at the place of the former Upper Castle, the whey health resort can be seen, which was erected after 1851. Today, the former place of serving goat´s milk – almost hidden by trees which have grown since – is the "Restaurant zur Molkenkur (Whey Cure Restaurant)". The castle, still today one of Germany´s foremost tourist attractions, presents itself unchanged to the observer. The Neckar having being canalized in the 1920s, however, forced the river into a straight bed.

Heidelberger Schloss (Heidelberg Castle), view from the North

Der achteckige Glockenturm des Heidelberger Schlosses vom Torturm aus gesehen um 1930. Links im Bild der Abgang zum Schlosskeller, in dem das bekannte „Große Fass“ aufgestellt ist.
Neben dem Schloss als touristische Hauptattraktion ist das große Fass heute eines der Hauptziele der internationalen Touristen und der Zwerg Perkeo, der einst das Fass der Sage nach leergetrunken haben soll, eines der bekanntesten Heidelberger „Originale“.

Der Glockenturm des Heidelberger Schlosses

The octagonal belfry of the Heidelberger Schloss, seen from the gate tower at about 1930. To the left there is the way down to the castle cellar, where the famous "Big Cask" is erected.

Besides the castle as a main attraction for tourists, today the cask is one of the main destinations of international tourists, and the dwarf Perkeo who according to the legend is said to have drunk the cask empty, is one of the most famous Heidelberg "characters".

The belfry of the Heidelberger Schloss

Der Torturm des Heidelberger Schlosses um 1900. Es ist das einzige unzerstörte Bauwerk des Schlosses. Der Torturm diente einst dem Torwächter als Wohnung und war Aufstellort der Turmuhr.
Obwohl baulich unverändert, hat der Torturm infolge der Entfernung seines ursprünglichen Bewuchses gegenüber dem früheren Charme etwas von seiner romantischen Ausstrahlung verloren.

Der Torturm
des Heidelberger Schlosses

The gate tower of the Heidelberger Schloss at about 1900. It is the only building of the castle which has remained undestroyed. Once the gate tower served as the guard´s accomodation and was the place where the tower clock was placed.
Although being unchanged as a building, due to taking away the original vegetation cover the gate tower has lost some of its romantic appeal if compared to its earlier charme.

The gate tower of the Heidelberger Schloss

Der kurfürstliche Marstall, aufgenommen nach einem Brand im Mai 1896, dem u.a. das Dach des Ostturmes (links) zum Opfer fiel. Der Bau des Neckarstadens, der die Hauptstraße vom Wagenverkehr entlasten sollte, ist noch nicht abgeschlossen. Seit 1921 beherbergt das Marstallgebäude eine Mensa. Links daneben ist die Heuscheuer zu erkennen, heute ein Hörsaalgebäude der Universität.
Dem heutigen Betrachter präsentiert sich der Marstall im wesentlichen unverändert, wenn auch in den Sommermonaten durch das dichte Grün der Natur verhüllt.

Blick auf den Marstall von Norden

The Elector´s "Marstall" (stable), photographed after a fire in May, 1896, to which among others the roof of the eastern tower (left) fell victim. The building of the "Neckarstaden", which was supposed the relieve the main street from wagon traffic, is not yet completed. Since 1921 the "Marstall" has been accomodating a university refectory. To its left the "Heuscheuer" (hay barn) can be recognized, today a lecture hall of the university.

To today´s observer the "Marstall" presents itself basically unchanged, if hidden by the dense green of nature during the summer months.

View at the "Marstall" from the North

Das Hotel „Zum Ritter“ ist das einzige Heidelberger Haus, dessen Fassade die Zerstörung der Stadt im 30jährigen Krieg und im Pfälzischen Erbfolgekrieg 1689/90 überdauert hat. Die historische Aufnahme entstand um 1900.
Seit 1681 als Gasthaus „Zum Ritter“ verzeichnet, steht der Renaissancebau von 1592 heute unter Denkmalschutz. Wo einst Tuchhändler ihre Geschäfte machten, schlafen heute Touristen in einem der schönsten historischen Hotelgebäude Heidelbergs.

Das Hotel „Zum Ritter“

The hotel "Zum Ritter" is the only house in Heidelberg whose front survived the destruction of the city in the Thirty Years War and the War of the Palatinate Succession 1689/90. This historic photography was taken at about 1900.
Listed as the guesthouse "Zum Ritter" since 1681, the Renaissance building from 1592 is under a preservation order today. There where cloth merchants once made their deals, tourists sleep in one of Heidelberg´s most beautiful hotel buildings today.

The hotel "Zum Ritter" (The Knight)

Die Bäckerei „Adams“ in der Unteren Straße 21, Ecke Dreikönigstraße. Links in der Tür steht die Bäckersfrau Else Adams.
Wie vor 100 Jahren dient das Haus auch heute noch als Bäckerei. Gegenwärtig unterhält die bekannte Heidelberger Bäckerei Mantei hier einen Filialbetrieb.

Blick auf die Bäckerei Adams

The "Adams" bakery at Untere Straße 21, at the corner of Dreikönigsstraße. Left from the door there stands the baker´s wife, Else Adams.

Just as 100 years ago, today the house still serves as a bakery. Currently the well-known Heidelberg Mantei bakery runs a branch here.

View at the "Adams" bakery

Am ersten Weihnachtsfeiertag 1919 tritt der Neckar wie so oft vor seiner Regulierung über die Ufer und verwandelt die Semmelgasse in eine Wasserstraße.

Wesentlich trockener als vor 100 Jahren präsentiert sich die Semmelgasse heute dem Auge des Betrachters. Renovierte Häuser und begrünte Fassaden werden nur noch selten vom Neckarhochwasser erreicht.

Blick in die überschwemmte Semmelgasse

On Christmas Day, 1919, as so often the Neckar once again breaks its banks and changes the Semmelgasse into a waterway.

Today the Semmelgasse presents itself to the observer in a much drier state than 100 years ago. Today renovated houses and fronts covered with greenery are only seldomly caught by the Neckar flood.

View at the Semmelgasse

Blick auf die Altstadt von Osten

Blick von Osten auf Stadt und Schloss. Zwei Brücken überqueren auf dieser Ansicht um 1900 den Neckar, 1928 kommt die Ernst-Walz-Brücke hinzu.

Während auf der südlichen Seite des Neckars die Heidelberger Altstadt nahezu unverändert erscheint, ist auf der Nordseite neben einem üppigeren Waldbewuchs heute auch eine dichtere und moderne Bebauung des Neckarufers auszumachen.

View at the city and the castle from the East. In this view from at about 1900 two bridges span the Neckar, in 1928 they are joined by the Ernst-Walz-Brücke.

Whereas on the southern banks of the Neckar the old part of the city looks almost unchanged, on the northern banks apart from dense woods the observer sees also that the Neckar banks are more densely and modern built.

View at the old part of the city from the East

Blick in die Hauptstraße am Universitätsplatz, um 1896 noch Ludwigsplatz. Rechts im Bild ein Wagen der 1885 eröffneten Pferdebahn.
Die Pferdebahn wurde 1902 von der elektrischen Straßenbahn abgelöst. Seit 1978 ist die Hauptstraße Fußgängerzone. Das den rechten Bildrand begrenzende Gebäude ist durch einen im Stil der Spätrenaissance 1900/01 errichteten Sandsteinbau ersetzt worden.

Hauptstraße am Universitätsplatz

View at Hauptstraße at the Universitätsplatz, at about 1896 still called Ludwigsplatz. The right part of the picture shows a wagon of the horse-drawn tram, established in 1885.
In 1902 the horse-drawn tram was replaced by the electric tram. Since 1978 the Hauptstraße is a pedestrians area. In 1900/01 the building at the right edge of the picture was replaced by a sandstone building erected in Late Renaissance style.

*Hauptstraße (Mainstreet)
at the Universitätsplatz
(University Square)*

Grabengasse,
Ecke Seminarstraße

Blick von der Grabengasse, Ecke Seminarstraße Richtung Universitätsplatz, aufgenommen 1913. Rechts das Gebäude der Stadtpost, vormals das reformierte Gymnasium.

Nach seinem Abriss 1932 entstand hier ein Seitenflügel der Neuen Universität. Gegenüber ist die schmucke Sandsteinfassade der Universitätsbibliothek zu erkennen, an die sich heute die Triplex-Mensa der Universität anschließt.

View from the Grabengasse, at the corner of Seminarstraße, towards Universitätsplatz, taken in 1913. To the right there is the building of the city post office, formerly the reformed grammar school. After it had been torn down in 1932, here a side wing of the New University was built. To the opposite, the handsome sandstone front of the university library can be recognized, where today there follows the Triplex refectory of the university.

Grabengasse, at the corner of Seminarstraße

Links im Bild die Peterskirche, die älteste Kirche Heidelbergs, erbaut um 1485. Rechts das Gebäude der Universitätsbibliothek. Foto um 1910.

Die Peterskirche

1864–70 wird die Kirche im neogotischen Stil umgebaut und erhält die feingliedrige Turmspitze. Etwa 100 Jahre später erfolgt der Rückbau. Der Turm wird mit einem Kupferdach ummantelt und bietet damit ein deutlich verändertes Bild. Am üppigen „Grün" hat sich dagegen wenig verändert.

In the left part of the picture there is Heidelberg´s Peterskirche, the city´s oldest church, built at about 1485. To the right there is the building of the university library. Photography from at about 1910.

1864–70 the church is rebuilt in Neo-Gothic style and is provided with its delicately made spire. About 100 years later there happens the re-reconstruction. The tower is covered by a copper roof and thus presents a clearly changed view. The lush "green", however, has hardly changed.

The Peterskirche (St. Peter´s Church)

Die Schiffsanlegestelle „Stadthalle"

Die Schiffsanlegestelle bei der Heidelberger Stadthalle um 1930 ist Ausgangspunkt für Ausflugsdampfer und Motorbootrundfahrten. Wer lieber auf eigene Faust unterwegs ist, kann sich ein Segel-, Paddel- oder Ruderboot leihen.

Noch heute halten an derselben Stelle die Heidelberger Ausflugsschiffe. Der Verleih von Einzelbooten ist mittlerweile jedoch eingestellt worden.

At about 1930 the berth at the Stadthalle is the place where pleasure steamers and motor boat trips start. Who prefers trips on his own may hire a sailing boat, a rowing boat, or a canoe.

Still today, Heidelberg´s pleasure ships stop at the same place. However, meanwhile the lending out of individual boats has come to an end.

The berth called "Stadthalle"

Alter OEG-Bahnhof

Das alte Bahnhofsgebäude der Oberrheinischen Eisenbahngesellschaft (OEG) am Bismarckplatz um 1929. Im Gebäude war auch die Polizeiwache integriert. Das Haus wurde noch im Jahr der Aufnahme abgerissen. Der heutige Betrachter kann sich beim Anblick dieser zwei Bilder nur mit Mühe in die 1920er Jahre zurückversetzen. Bus- und Straßenbahnhaltestellen bestimmen nunmehr das Bild des Platzes. 1955 gibt die OEG auch ihr Verwaltungsgebäude am Bismarckplatz auf (Gebäude links im Bild, hinter dem Blumenkiosk). An dieser Stelle befindet sich heute das Kaufhaus Woolworth.

The old station building of the Oberrheinische Eisenbahngesellschaft (OEG) at the Bismarckplatz at about 1929. The house was torn down already in that same year. When looking at these two pictures, today´s observer will find it difficult to imagine the 1920s. Now the image of the square is dominated by bus and tram stations. In 1955 the OEG also abandones its administration building at the Bismarckplatz (the building in the left part of the picture, behind the flower kiosk). Today, at this place there is the Woolworth department store.

Old OEG station

Der Bismarckplatz

Der Bismarckplatz, ein wichtiger Verkehrsknotenpunkt; und das bereits 1929. Die Ansiedlung mehrerer Hotels – links im Bild das Hotel „Reichspost“, rechts das Hotel „Bayrischer Hof“ – ergibt sich aus der günstigen Lage nahe des Alten Hauptbahnhofs.

Während das einstige Gebäude des Hotels „Reichspost“ mittlerweile einem modernen Warenhaus gewichen ist, blieb der „Bayrische Hof“ erhalten. Das Befahren den Platzes ist heute allein dem ÖPNV vorbehalten.

The Bismarckplatz, an important traffic junction, and that as early as in 1929. The establishment of several hotels – in the left part of the picture the "Reichspost" hotel, to the right the "Bayerischer Hof" hotel – is due to the favourable location near the Old Main Station.

Whereas meanwhile the former building of the "Reichspost" hotel has been replaced by a modern department store, the "Bayerische Hof" has been preserved. Today, only the ÖPNV (passenger transportation) is entitled to drive on the square.

The Bismarckplatz

Der Alte Bahnhof unweit des Bismarckplatzes trennt mit seinen Gleisanlagen die im Hintergrund sichtbare Weststadt vom Stadtzentrum und Bergheim. 1955 wird er nach Westen verlegt. Die Stadtteile Bergheim und Weststadt können nun zusammenwachsen.

Als Ausdruck moderner Stadtentwicklung entsteht auf dem ehemaligen Bahnhofsareal der Menglerbau – das nach seinem Architekten benannte einzige Hochhaus in der Heidelberger Innenstadt – mit angeschlossenem Einkaufszentrum. Dessen Fassade freilich ist hinter den im Sommer wohltuenden Schatten spendenden Bäumen nahezu verdeckt.

Alter Heidelberger Bahnhof

The Alte Heidelberger Bahnhof not far away from the Bismarckplatz with its track system separates the Western City, to be seen in the background, from the city centre and Bergheim. In 1955 it is moved to the West. Now the districts of Bergheim and Western City can grow into one. As an expression of modern urban development the Mengler Building – the only tower block in Heidelberg´s inner city, named after the architect and including a shopping centre – is built on the area of the former station. Its front, however, is almost completely covered by trees which in the summer afford pleasant shade.

Alter Heidelberger Bahnhof (Old Heidelberg Station)

Die alte Hauptpost

Die alte Hauptpost in der Rohrbacher Straße. 1876 erbaut, wurde sie 1910 um ein viertes Stockwerk erweitert, um den zunehmenden Telefon- und Telegraphenverkehr bewältigen zu können.
Bei Tiefbauarbeiten für das neue Kaufhaus am Bismarckplatz wird das Postgebäude in seinen Grundfesten erschüttert. Auf Grund statischer Probleme muss es 1974, nach dem Umzug der Hauptpost in einen Neubau in der Belfortstraße, abgerissen werden. 1976 entsteht ein Geschäftsneubau mit gemischter Nutzung, der in seiner Anmutung nicht mit dem Vorgängerbau konkurrieren kann.

The Alte Hauptpost in Rohrbacher Straße. Built in 1876, it was extended by a fourth storey in 1910 to be able to cope with increasing telephone and telegraph communication.

In the course of groundwork for the new department store at the Bismarckplatz the foundations of the post office building are shaken. In 1974, after the Hauptpost has moved to a new building in Belfortstraße, it must be torn down due to statics problems. In 1976 a new business building for mixed purposes is built, whose presentation cannot compete with the preceding building.

The Alte Hauptpost (Old General Post Office)

Das Stadtgartenrestaurant

Das Stadtgartenrestaurant im Heidelberger Stadtgarten, eröffnet 1886, ist ein beliebter Ort für öffentliche Konzerte und gesellige Veranstaltungen. Der umgebende Stadtgarten ist als Oase der Ruhe geschätzt und bekannt. Foto um 1900.

Noch heute ist das Restaurant im Stadtgarten bei den Heidelbergern beliebt. Der erste Neubau des Hauses – in weitaus schlichteren Formen – entstand kurz nach dem alten Bild im Jahr 1911. Das Haus wurde nach einem Brand (2002) im Jahr 2005 wiedererrichtet.

The Stadtgarten restaurant in the Heidelberg Stadtpark (City Park), opened up in 1886, is a popular place of public concerts and social meetings. The surrounding Stadtgarten is well-known and appreciated as an oasis of quietness. Photography from at about 1900.

Still today, the restaurant in the Stadtgarten is popular among the inhabitants of Heidelberg. The first new building of the house – much more modest – was erected shortly after this old picture in 1911. After having burned down (2002) the house was built again in 2005.

The Stadtgarten restaurant

Die Kastanienallee in der Leopoldanlage

Die großzügig mit einer Kastanienallee gestaltete Leopoldanlage ist eine der Hauptverkehrsachsen Heidelbergs. Sie entsteht parallel zum Ausbau der Trasse der Odenwaldbahn. Die repräsentativen Wohn- und Geschäftshäuser stammen vorwiegend aus der Zeit Ende des 19. Jahrhunderts.

Die Kastanien sind der heutigen Friedrich-Ebert-Anlage erhalten geblieben. Dennoch wirkt sie nicht mehr so beschaulich wie um 1914, der Autoverkehr hat dem Erscheinungsbild seinen Stempel aufgedrückt.

The Leopoldanlage, lavishly provided with a chestnut avenue, is one of Heidelberg´s main traffic axes. It is built parallel to constructing the tracks of the Odenwaldbahn (Odenwald Railway). The prestigious residential and business buildings date mostly from the end of the 19th century.

The chestnut trees have been preserved as a part of today´s Friedrich-Ebert-Anlage. Nevertheless, it does not look as peaceful anymore as at about 1914, its image is now characterized by car traffic.

The Kastanienallee in the Leopoldanlage

Der Wredeplatz

Marktgeschehen auf dem Wredeplatz um 1900. Heidelberg, die Geburtsstadt von Karl Philipp von Wrede, erhielt das 12.846 Gulden teure Denkmal des Feldmarschalls als Geschenk vom bayrischen König. 1940 wird die Bronzestatue eingeschmolzen.
Bis in die Gegenwart finden Markttage auf dem heutigen Friedrich-Ebert-Platz statt. Außerhalb dieser Zeiten dient er als innerstädtischer Parkplatz. Das Bauschild kündigt die anstehende Neugestaltung des Platzes mit der in der Öffentlichkeit umstrittenen Entfernung der 1927 erbauten Marktkolonaden an, die den Blick auf das ehemalige Chemische Institut, in dem Robert Bunsen arbeitete, verstellen (Aufnahme September 2007).

Market business on the Wredeplatz at about 1900. Heidelberg, Karl Philipp von Wrede´s city of birth, was given the memorial of the fieldmarshall, which cost 12.846 guilders, as a present from the King of Bavaria. In 1940 the bronze statue is melted down.
Still today there are market days on what is today the Friedrich-Ebert-Platz. Otherwise it is used as an inner-city car park. The sign announces the imminent restructuring of the square by taking away the market collonades built in 1927 – a publicly debated step – which block the view at the former Chemical Institute where Robert Bunsen worked (photography from September, 2007).

The Wredeplatz

Angeregt durch die provisorische Festhalle zum Universitätsjubiläum 1886 planen die Heidelberger Bürger den Bau eines soliden Gebäudes an gleicher Stelle. Der Stadthallenbau kostet über 1 Million Mark. 1903 erfolgt die Einweihung. Seither werden hier Feste gefeiert, Konzerte und Ausstellungen besucht und Konferenzen abgehalten.

Die historische Aufnahme von 1930 bietet dem Betrachter von heute einen fast unveränderten Anblick. Dabei trennt die mittlerweile vom Durchgangs- und Pendlerverkehr sehr frequentierte Uferstraße die Stadthalle vom Fluss. Aber es gibt Planungen, die unter dem Stichwort „Stadt am Fluss“ die unterirdische Verkehrsführung und moderne Erweiterung des Stadthallenkomplexes vorsehen, um die künstliche Trennung wieder aufzuheben.

Die Stadthalle

Stimulated by the provisionary festival hall for the university´s anniversary in 1886, the citizens of Heidelberg intend to build a solid building at the same place. The building of the Stadthalle costs more than 1 million Marks. In 1903 it is officially opened. Since then it has been the place of celebrations, concerts, exhibitions, and congresses.

This historic photography from 1930 presents today´s observer with an almost unchanged view. However, the Uferstraße, which meanwhile is heavily used by commuters and through traffic, separates the Stadthalle from the river. Under the keyword "city on the river" there are thoughts of establishing an underground traffic system and a modern extension of the Stadthalle complex, in order of abandoning again this artificial separation.

The Stadthalle (Festival Hall)

Die Hauptstraße

Die Heidelberger Hauptstraße 1899, noch mit den Schienen der Pferdebahn. Links die Gastwirtschaft „Zur goldenen Gerste". Das Gebäude mit dem Säuleneingang ist das 1712 erbaute Palais Morass, seit 1908 Sitz der Städtischen Kunst- und Altertümersammlung (heute Kurpfälzisches Museum).

Die „Goldene Gerste" ist mittlerweile von einer irischen Gastwirtschaft abgelöst worden, und auch die Pferdebahn zieht ihre Bahnen nicht mehr durch die Heidelberger Hauptstraße, selbst wenn ihre einstige Gleisführung durch die neue Pflasterung fast nachgeahmt scheint.

The Heidelberg Mainstreet in 1899, still showing the tracks of the horse-drawn tram. To the left there is the pub "Zur Goldenen Gerste (Golden Barley)" The building with the columned entrance is the Palais Morass, built in 1712, after 1908 the seat of the city´s art and antiques collection (today the Kurpfälzisches Museum).

Meanwhile the "Goldene Gerste" has been replaced by an Irish pub, and also the horse-drawn tram does not appear anymore in Mainstreet, even if its former tracks seem to be almost imitated by the modern road surface.

The Hauptstraße (Mainstreet)

Blick in die Hauptstraße um 1900. Rechts die Providenzkirche, im Hintergrund der Turm der Heiliggeistkirche. Die Fachgeschäfte und Restaurants zeigen ein durchaus belebtes Straßenbild. In diesem Bereich der Hauptstraße waren die Schienen der Pferdebahn zweigleisig verlegt.
Deutlich geschäftiger erscheint die Heidelberger Hauptstraße nach ihrer Umwandlung in eine Fußgängerzone 1978. Zeittypische Renovierungen haben die Häuser oft ihrer einstigen Dekorationen wie Lampen und Schilder beraubt, sie strahlen bisweilen eher geschäftsmäßige Konformität aus.

View at Mainstreet at about 1900. To the right there is the Provinzkirche (Province Church), in the background the steeple of the Heiliggeistkirche (Holy Spirit Church). The shops and restaurants show a definitely lively image. In this part of Mainstreet the horse-drawn tram was double-tracked. After having been changed into a pedestrian area in 1978, Mainstreet looks much more busy. Often ways of renovation which were typical for that time have deprived the houses of their former decorations, such as lamps and signs, and now they sometimes express rather businesslike conformity.

Der Universitätsplatz

Der Universitätsplatz – früher Ludwigsplatz – wird wiederholt umgestaltet. Zur Zeit der historischen Aufnahme (1908) ziert das Reiterdenkmal von Kaiser Wilhelm I. die Platzmitte. Es wird im März 1918 demontiert und zu Kriegszwecken eingeschmolzen. Links im Bild ein Flügel des Gebäudes der Alten Universität. Das Gebäude rechts im Bild ist der 1828 eingeweihte Weinbrennerbau, ursprünglich Sitz der Museumsgesellschaft. Es dient seit 1901 als Neues Kollegienhaus der Universität. Der amerikanische Botschafter Jakob Gould Schurman, ehemaliger Student in Heidelberg, finanziert mit in USA gesammelten Spendengeldern Anfang der 1930er Jahre den Bau der Neuen Universität, die heute auf dem Areal des Weinbrennerbaus steht.

The Universitätsplatz – formerly Ludwigsplatz – has repeatedly been restructured. At the time of this historic photography (1917) the horse statue of Emperor William I. decorates the centre of the square. In March, 1918, it is pulled down and melted down for war purposes. In the left part of the picture there is a wing of the Old University building. The building in the right part of the picture there is the Weinbrennerbau, officially opened in 1828, and originally the seat of the Museum Society. Under the name of Neues Kollegienhaus it has been used by the university since 1901. At the beginning of the 1930s the American ambassador, Jakob Gould Schurman, a former university student in Heidelberg, funded the building of the New University by funds raised in the USA, which today is on the area of the Weinbrennerhaus.

The Universitätsplatz (University Square)

Der Heumarkt mit Blick auf die Häuserzeile der Großen Mantelgasse. Die mittelständischen Wohn- und Geschäftshäuser sind direkt an die ehemalige Stadtmauer gebaut.

Obschon die Gebäude sich in durchaus sehenswertem Zustand präsentieren und Cafés und Restaurants zum Verweilen auf dem mittelalterlichen Platz etwas Abseits der belebten Hauptstraße einladen, deutet sich mit den geparkten Drahteseln und Autos doch auch die bisweilen in der Altstadt herrschende Enge an.

Heumarkt/Große Mantelgasse

The Heumarktplatz, view at the rows of houses of the Große Mantelgasse. These middle class residential and business buildings were built immediately at the old city wall.

Although the buildings present themselves in a state which is definitely worth seeing and cafés and restaurants invite for a stay at this medieval square which is somewhat away from busy Mainstreet, nevertheless parked bycicles and cars sometimes indicate the narrowness of Heidelberg´s old part of the city.

Heumarkt (Haymarket)/ Große Mantelgasse

Alltag in der Kleinen Mantelgasse, eine der Gassen zwischen Hauptstraße und Neckar, in der eine bunte Mischung aus Handwerkern, Lohnarbeitern und Kleingewerbetreibenden wohnt. Schuhmacher und Kleidermacher, ein Schreibmaschinenbureau und ein Eiergeschäft „leben“ in der Nachbarschaft zu Laternenwärter, Ausläufer und Büglerin.
Die Häuser der Kleinen Mantelgasse haben von der Sanierung der Altstadt sehr profitiert und sind auch heute wieder begehrter Wohnraum.

Kleine Mantelgasse

Everyday scenery in the Kleine Mantelgasse, one of the streets between Mainstreet and the Neckar, where there lives a colourful mixture of craftsmen, workers, and small traders. Shoemakers and taylors, a typewriter office, and an egg store "live" next door with lamp attendant, "Ausläufer", and ironing woman.

The houses of the Kleine Mantelgasse have much benefitted from the renovation of the old part of the city and today they are a much demanded residential area again.

Kleine Mantelgasse

Studenten vor dem Café „Knösel“ in der Unteren Straße, im Volksmund auch bekannt als „Café Studentenkuss“. Das Haus wurde 1704 als Wohn- und Geschäftshaus erbaut. Schnell avancierte das Café nach 1863 zu einem beliebten Treffpunkt der Bürger, Professoren und zahlreicher Studenten. 1903 erwarben Caroline Knösel und ihr Mann das Haus und machten daraus die Heimat des berühmten „Studentenkusses“, einer Spezialität, die aus einem feinen Waffelboden mit Nugatbelag und Zartbitterumhüllung besteht. Auch nach dem Verkauf des Hauses durch die Familie Knösel im Jahr 2005 findet sich hier ein beliebtes Café in der Heidelberger Altstadt, eines der ältesten zudem.

Das Café „Knösel“

University students in front of the "Knösel" café in the Untere Straße, commonly also known as "Student´s Kiss Café". In 1704 the house was built as a residential and business building. After 1883 the café quickly grew to become a popular meeting place of citizens, professors, and many students. In 1903 Caroline Knösel and her husband bought the house and made it the home of the famous "Student´s Kiss", a speciality of the house consisting of a fine wafer with a nougat topping and a covering of dark chocolate. Even after the house was sold by the Knösel family in 2005 it is a popular café in Heidelberg´s old part, and also one of the oldest ones.

The Knösel café

Droschkenanstalt Karl Seppich

Stolze Kutscher posieren 1910 vor der Droschkenanstalt Karl Seppich in der Dreikönigstraße. Gerne lassen sich die Studenten von den livrierten Kutschern zu ihren Festen fahren.

Der Betrieb der Familie Seppich hat sich bis heute in der Heidelberger Altstadt erhalten. Während die Pferde längst dem Ottomotor als Antriebsmittel gewichen sind, können sich noch heute nicht nur Studenten dort Leihfahrzeuge mieten; doch müssen sie diese dann selbst chauffieren.

In 1910 proud coachmen pose in front of the Droschkenanstalt Karl Seppich in the Dreikönigstraße. University students like to be driven to their parties by the liveried coachmen.

Still today the company of the Seppich family is existent in Heidelberg´s old part. Whereas the horses have long been replaced by the Otto engine, still today not only university students may hire a car there, but they must chauffeur themselves.

Droschkenanstalt (Coach Company) Karl Seppich

Der renommierte Gasthof „Goldener Hecht" und die Kolonialwarenhandlung „Stauch" begrüßten schon vor 100 Jahren die Reisenden am ehemaligen Stadteingang zur Altstadt.

Aber auch noch heute genießen die Hotelgäste im „Goldenen Hecht" den malerischen Blick auf den Neckar und die Brücke. Im einstigen Kolonialwarenladen, heute mit ausgebautem Dachgeschoss, werden – Heidelberg ist mittlerweile international – asiatische Köstlichkeiten angeboten.

Steingasse/„Goldener Hecht"

Already 100 years ago the renowned guesthouse "Goldener Hecht" and the "Stauch" grocer´s shop greeted travellers at the former gate to the old part of the city.

But still today the hotel guests at the "Golden Hecht" enjoy the pittoresque view at the Neckar and the bridge. At the former grocer´s shop, today with a converted attic, Asian delikatessen are offered today – Heidelberg has meanwhile become international.

Steingasse/
"Goldener Hecht (Golden Pike)"

Blick von der Alten Brücke auf die Heidelberger Altstadt und das Schloss um 1900. Stadt am Fluss. Kinder werden zu Wasserratten, vorn rechts im Bild ist der alte Schlachthof zu sehen.

Blick von der Alten Brücke

Doch mit der Ruhe und Beschaulichkeit einer größeren Freifläche ist es vorbei: Wo früher das Vieh getränkt und geschlachtet wurde, pulsiert heute der Verkehr über den 1897 eingeweihten Neckarstaden auf der Ost-West-Schiene entlang des Neckars.

View from the Alte Brücke at Heidelberg´s old part and the castle at about 1900. City on the river. Children become keen swimmers, to the right fore of the picture the old slaughterhouse can be seen.

But the quietness and peace of a wide free space has come to an end: there where in the old days cattle was watered and slaughtered, today there rushes traffic on the Neckarstaden, officially opened in 1897, on the East-West axis along the Neckar.

View from the Alte Brücke (Old Bridge)

Wochenmarkt auf dem Marktplatz vor der Heiliggeistkirche. Der Markt fand um 1900 in den Monaten April bis September jeweils am Montag, Mittwoch, Donnerstag und Samstag statt. Die Buden zwischen den Pfeilern der Kirche haben eine jahrhundertealte Tradition.
Unverändert präsentiert sich die Heiliggeistkirche von Osten gesehen dem heutigen Betrachter. Während in den Buden an der Kirche heute überwiegend Reiseandenken feilgeboten werden, dominieren die Straßencafés mit vielen Heidelberg-Touristen das Bild des Marktplatzes.

Wochenmarkt vor der Heiliggeistkirche

Weekly market in front of the Heiliggeistkirche. At about 1900 market day was from April to September on every Monday, Wednesday, Thursday, and Saturday. The cabins between the pillars of the church look back to a centuries old tradition.
Unchanged, the Heiliggeistkirche presents itself to today´s observer, seen from the East. Whereas today mostly travel souvenirs are offered at the cabins near the church, the image of the market square is dominated by street cafés with many Heidelberg tourists.

Weekly market in front of the Heiliggeistkirche

Das Heidelberger Rathaus

Das Heidelberger Rathaus wurde mehrfach umgebaut und erweitert. Zwei Bürgerhäuser flankierten ursprünglich den 1701/1703 errichteten barocken Mittelbau. Das ehemalige Gasthaus zum Goldenen Hirsch (im Bild links) wurde für die Rathauserweiterung abgerissen. Der Dachstuhlbrand im Mittelbau 1908 forcierte die weiteren Umbauplanungen. In den 1920er Jahren hat das Gebäudeensemble mit der neobarocken Erweiterung zur Hauptstraße hin sein heutiges Gesicht erhalten.

Heidelberg´s Rathaus has been converted and extended several times. Originally, the baroque central building, erected in 1701/1703, was flanked by two upper middle class houses.

The former guesthouse "Goldener Hirsch (Golden Stag)" (in the left part of the picture) was torn down for the extension of the city hall. In 1908 a fire in the attic increased further plans of restructuring. In the 1920s, by the neo-baroque extension towards Mainstreet the ensemble of buildings was given its current look.

Heidelberger Rathaus (City Hall)

Das 1701 erbaute Gebäude der kurfürstlichen Hofapotheke ist nach der Zerstörung Heidelbergs 1689 und 1693 eines der frühesten Barockgebäude in der Altstadt. Um 1910 präsentierte darin das Kaufhaus Methlow Herren- und Damenmoden, hielt mit dem Warenhaus gleichsam großstädtisches Flair seinen Einzug in Heidelberg.
Heute werden in dem renovierten Geschäftsgebäude Tourismusandenken vor allem für Heidelbergbesucher aus Fernost verkauft.

Kurfürstliche Hofapotheke

After the destruction of Heidelberg in 1689 and 1693 the building of the elector´s court pharmacy, built in 1701, is one of the earliest baroque buildings in the old part of the city. At about 1910, there the Methlow department store presented men´s and women´s fashion, with this department store an air of big cities was introduced to Heidelberg, so to speak.
Today at the renovated business building mostly touristic souveniers are sold to visitors to Heidelberg from the Far East.

Kurfürstliche Hofapotheke
(The Elector´s Court harmacy)

Blick auf den Heidelberger Kornmarkt und das Schloss um 1900. Auf dem Kornmarkt die „Madonna Immaculata" von 1718. Die Kutschen im Vordergrund dienten häufig Touristen als Gefährt für Stadtrundfahrten.

Bis auf den Ausbau einiger Dachstühle und den Rückbau des markanten Türmchens am Eckgebäude präsentiert sich der Kornmarkt heute fast unverändert den Besuchern. Auch beim Anblick des Schlosses scheint die Zeit stehen geblieben zu sein.

Kornmarkt

View at Heidelberg´s grain market square and the castle at about 1900. On the grain market square there is the "Madonna Immaculata" from 1718. Often the coaches in the foreground served tourists as vehicles for sightseeing tours.

Apart from some attics having been converted and the striking small steeple of the corner building having been re-converted, today the grain market square presents itself almost unchanged to the observer. Also in respect of the view of the castle time seems to stand still.

Kornmarkt
(Grain Market)

Hotel „Prinz Carl“

Das Hotel „Prinz Carl“ am Kornmarkt, entstanden 1785–88, avancierte im 19. Jahrhundert zu einem der renommiertesten Hotels der Stadt. So nächtigten hier unter anderem Bismarck, Moltke, Jules Verne und Graf Zeppelin. Gehobene Kreise der Heidelberger Bürgerschaft trafen sich zu geselligen Abenden und Feiern im auch heute noch erhaltenen Spiegelsaal. 1915 wurde das Hotel geschlossen und zunächst zum Reservelazarett umfunktioniert.

Nach dem Verkauf des Gebäudes an die Stadt Heidelberg beherbergt der Prinz Carl seit 1919 Teile der Stadtverwaltung. Aufgrund gravierender Bauschäden erfolgte der Abriss des historischen Gebäudes, um 1990 der Öffentlichkeit einen wieder aufgebauten Prinz Carl zu übergeben.

In the course of the 19th century the "Prinz Carl" hotel at the grain market square, established 1785–88, grew to become one of the city´s most renowned hotels. Accordingly, among others Bismarck, Moltke, Jules Verne, and Count Zeppelin stayed there for the night. For sociable evenings and celebrations the better part of Heidelberg´s society met in the Mirror Hall which is preserved still today. In 1915 the hotel was closed down and at first changed into an army hospital. After the building had been sold to the City of Heidelberg, since 1919 Prinz Carl accomodates part of the municipal administration. Due to grave building damages, the historic building was torn down, to present a newly erected "Prinz Carl" to the public in 1990.

The "Prinz Carl" hotel

Das Karlstor am östlichen Ende der Altstadt wurde in den Jahren von 1775 bis 1781 in Anlehnung an das römische Triumphbogenmotiv errichtet. Mit dem Torbau bedankte sich die Heidelberger Bürgerschaft bei Kurfürst Karl Theodor für die erfahrene Förderung.

Mittlerweile sind die auf dem 1937 aufgenommenen Foto noch erkennbaren Schienen der Straßenbahn längst verschwunden, ebenso die Buden im Vordergrund und die Nebengebäude des alten Bahnhofs. Dagegen hat das Karlstor selbst durch einen breiteren Grünstreifen sichtbar mehr Distanz zum lärmenden Verkehr gewonnen.

Das Karlstor

The Karlstor at the eastern end of the old part of the city was erected between 1775 and 1781, while following the model of Roman triumphal arches. Building this gate was the Heidelberg citizens´ way of saying thank you to Elector Karl Theodor for his support.

Meanwhile the tracks of the tram, which are still to be seen on this photography from 1937, have long gone. The same is true for the cabins in the foreground and the outbuildings of the old train station. On the other hand, the Karlstor itself has visibly more distance to the traffic noise, due to a broad grass verge.

The Karlstor (Karl´s Gate)

Einer der bekanntesten Blicke auf Heidelberg. Stadt am Fluss: Altstadt, Schloss, Alte Brücke und Heiliggeistkirche vom Philosophenweg aus gesehen.

Das rechts neben dem Torturm bestehende Café Bolley wurde im Zusammenhang mit der Erweiterung der Uferstraße abgerissen. Der 1897 errichtete und stark befahrene Neckarstaden trennt Altstadt und den Neckar. Und dennoch präsentiert sich noch heute und durch den Krieg nahezu unzerstört Heidelbergs bekanntester Blick auf Altstadt und Schloss dem Bildbetrachter.

Blick vom Philosophenweg

One of the most famous views at Heidelberg. City on the river: old part, castle, Old Bridge, and Heiliggeistkirche, seen from the Philosophenberg.
Café Bolley, which is seen to the right of the gate tower, was torn down in the context of extenting the Uferstraße. The Neckarstaden with much traffic on it, which was built in 1897, separates the old part of the city from the Neckar. But nevertheless, still today the observer is presented with the most famous view at Heidelberg´s old part and the castle, almost undestroyed by the war.

View from the Philosophenberg (Philosopher´s Mountain)

Die Friedrichsbrücke, jetzt Theodor-Heuss-Brücke

Die neue Heidelberger Neckarbrücke verdankt ihre Entstehung vor allem dem Wunsch vieler Gemeinden von Neuenheim bis Weinheim nach einer schnelleren Erreichbarkeit des Heidelberger Bahnhofs. 1877 wird die Friedrichsbrücke feierlich eröffnet und 1906 aufgrund der zunehmenden Mobilität und zum Einbau wichtiger Versorgungsleitungen für Gas, Wasser und Elektrizität verbreitert. Links im Bild ist die 1903 eröffnete Stadthalle zu erkennen, auf der Neckarwiese wird noch Wäsche „geblichen".

Die Friedrichsbrücke wird am Kriegsende von der Deutschen Wehrmacht auf dem Rückzug gesprengt und 1949 erstmals sowie 1992 erneut durch eine neue Brückenkonstruktion ersetzt. 1964 wird die Friedrichsbrücke in Theodor-Heuss-Brücke umbenannt. Sie ist heute mehr denn je wichtige Verkehrsverbindung auf der Nord-Süd-Achse und hat eine hohe infrastrukturelle Bedeutung für die Anbindung der nördlichen Stadtteile Neuenheim und Handschuhsheim.

Heidelberg´s new bridge over the Neckar is most of all due to the wish of many communities, from Neuenheim as far as to Weinheim, to be faster connected to the Heidelberg train station. In 1877 the Friedrichsbrücke is ceremonially opened, and in 1906 it is widened beacuse of increasing mobility and the installation of important pipes and cables for gas, water, and electricity. In the left part of the picture the Stadthalle, opened in 1903, can be recognized, it is still common to "bleach" washing on the meadow near the Neckar.

At the end of World War II the Friedrichsbrücke is blown up by the Wehrmacht during its retreat and in 1949 it is for the first time replaced by a new construction, as well as a second time in 1992. In 1964 the Friedrichsbrücke is renamed in Theodor-Heuss-Brücke. More than ever, it is an important connection at the North-South axis today and is of high infrastructural significance for connecting the northern districts of Neuenheim and Handschuhsheim.

The Friedrichsbrücke,
now Theodor-Heuss-Brücke

Das repräsentative Mannheimer Tor markiert im 19. Jahrhundert den westlichen Abschluss der Heidelberger Hauptstraße. Mit dem nach 1840 beginnenden Eisenbahnzeitalter nimmt die Stadtentwicklung über die Altstadt und den das Tor umgebenden Platz hinaus ihren Anfang. Das Tor wird als Hindernis empfunden und 1856 abgerissen.
Heute prägt den Platz vor allem seine Funktion als Drehscheibe des öffentlichen Personennahverkehrs. Fußgänger strömen in die Altstadt. Der Platz gleicht einem Nadelöhr inmitten des heftig pulsierenden Verkehrs. Seit 1985 steht an der Stelle des früheren Tores die moderne Plastik des Künstlerehepaars Martin Matschinsky und Brigitte Meier-Denninghoff für die Funktion des Bismarckplatzes als zentralem Verkehrskotenpunkt in Heidelberg. Zwei einander annähernd spiegelsymmetrisch zugeordnete Stränge verweisen auf die vier Hauptverkehrsachsen.

Das Mannheimer Tor

In the 19th century the prestigious Mannheimer Tor marks the western connection to Heidelberg´s Mainstreet. With the age of the railroad, starting after 1840, urban development beyond the old part and the square around the gate begins. The gate is considered an obstacle and is torn down in 1856. Today the square is most of all characterized by its function as a hub of passenger transportation. There is a stream of pedestrians on their way to the old part of the city. The square is a narrow passage in the midst of heavy traffic. Since 1985, at the place of the former gate a modern sculpture by the artist couple Martin Matschinsky and Brigitte Meier-Denninghoff represents the function of the Bismarckplatz as a central traffic connection in Heidelberg. Two almost mirror-symmetrically organized skeins symbolize the four main traffic axes.

The Mannheimer Tor (Mannheim Gate)

Der Schlachthof

Der 1893 eröffnete Heidelberger Schlachthof in der Bergheimer Straße 153 bringt um 1900 viel Bewegung und Leben in das Bergheimer Straßenbild. Die Metzger aus der Stadt kommen mit auf die Spurweite der Straßenbahn angepassten Handwagen oder mit Landauern zum Schlachthof. Auf dem Areal findet sich auch eine Gastwirtschaft, die für gutes und reichliches Essen bekannt ist.

Die Gebäude des 1954 stillgelegten Heidelberger Schlachthofs werden seit 1958 durch die Heidelberger Straßen- und Bergbahn AG genutzt. Vor allem die Hallen sind als Omnibusdepot und Werkstätten um- bzw. ausgebaut.

At about 1900 Heidelberg´s slaughterhouse at Bergheimer Straße 153, opened in 1893, makes the image of Bergheim much more lively. Butchers from all over the city come with their handcarts which are adjusted to the tracks of the tram or with "Landauers" (a four-wheeled coach with four seats). On the area there is also a pub which is famous for good and rich meals.

Since 1958 the buildings of Heidelberg´s slaughterhouse, which was closed down in 1954, have been used by the Heidelberger Straßen- und Bergbahn AG. Most of all the halls have been converted or extended to serve as bus depots and garages.

The Slaughterhouse

Blick in die Bergheimer Straße in westlicher Richtung. Zahlreiche Einzelhandelsgeschäfte von der Bäckerei bis zum Kolonialwarenladen und Gastwirtschaften prägen das Straßenbild ebenso wie die Vorgärten.
Der stetig wachsende Verkehr bedingt in den Jahren 1952–54 die Verbreiterung der Straße. Die Straßenbahn ist nun in einem eigenen Gleisbett unterwegs. Der Charakter als Wohn- und Einkaufsstraße hat sich weitgehend erhalten, wenn auch die Trennwirkung der Straße durch die Funktion als Haupterschließungsachse und die daraus resultierende überdurchschnittlich hohe Verkehrsbelastung nicht unerheblich sind.

Die Bergheimer Straße

View at the Bergheimer Straße to the West. Many shops, from a bakery as far as to a grocer´s, as well as pubs characterize the image of the street and the front gardens. Between 1952 and 1954 the constantly increasing traffic forces the street to be widened. Now the tram goes on tracks of its own. The street´s nature of being a residential and shopping street has mostly been preserved, even if due to its function as a main axis and resulting heavy traffic, which is above average, the street has quite a separating effect.

Das Bild zeigt die Steubenstraße im 1903 eingemeindeten Stadtteil Handschuhsheim. Der Stadtteil entwickelt sich im späten 19. Jahrhundert zum Einzugsgebiet der Stadt. An den Straßenzügen, in denen wie hier seit 1912 die Straßenbahn verläuft, breiten sich in den 1920er Jahren Wohn- und Geschäftsbauten aus. Mit der barockisierenden Gestaltung des Wohnblocks Steubenstr. 74–76 wird im Sozialwohnungsbau in Heidelberg historische Formensprache mit modernem Wohnkomfort verbunden.

Dieser Straßenzug präsentiert sich auch heute noch ganz ähnlich: Die Bahntrasse ist inzwischen verlegt, der Grahampark mit prachtvollem alten Baumbestand rechts erinnert an die blühende englische Kolonie in Heidelberg und Handschuhsheim. Im Hintergrund ist der Turm der St.-Vitus-Kirche zu sehen. Reste der östlichen Turmmauer gehen auf die im 11. Jahrhundert im romanischen Baustil gebaute Kirche zurück.

Handschuhsheim

The picture shows the Steubenstraße in the district of Handschuhsheim which became part of the city in 1903. In the late 19th century the districts develops to be part of the city´s environment. Along those streets where the tram goes after 1912 there spread residential and business buildings in the 1920s. In Heidelberg, by designing the block of flats of Steubenstraße 74–76 in a baroquicizing way historic forms and modern comfort of homes are combined.

Still today, this street presents itself quite similarly: the railroad tracks have meanwhile been moved, the Graham Park to the right with its beautiful old trees reminds to the flourishing British colony in Heidelberg and Handschuhsheim. In the background the steeple of St. Vitus´s Church can be seen. Remnants of the eastern tower wall reach back to the church built in Romanic style in the 11th century.

Handschuhsheim

Der Kohlhof

Die Hotel-Pension „Kohlhof" wurde im Jahr 1890 im Heidelberger Stadtwald eröffnet, „um den Einheimischen in nächster Nähe Erholung zu gewähren". Das Kurhotel in der Naturidylle in 430 Metern Höhe erwirbt sich schnell einen ausgezeichneten Ruf. Schon damals wurde auch auf Kinderfreundlichkeit geachtet, sogar eine „Kinderspielhalle" wurde im neuen Hotel eingerichtet.

An Stelle des nach wie vor beliebten Ausflugsziels der Heidelberger steht heute die Rehabilitationsklinik Heidelberg-Königsstuhl, eine Fachklinik für Innere Medizin, Herz- und Kreislaufkrankheiten.

The "Kohlhof" hotel and guesthouse was opened in Heidelberg´s Stadtwald in 1890, "to offer recreation to the inhabitants of the city close to their homes". Quickly this health spa resort, located in the midst of idyllic nature 430 m above sea level, gains outstanding reputation. Even in those days there was paying attention to providing a children-friendly atmosphere, even a "playing hall for children" was established at the new hotel. Today, at the place of this still very popular destination of outings there is the Heidelberg-Königsstuhl rehabilitation clinics, a special hospital for internal medicine and heart-circulatory illnesses.

The Kohlhof

Die Friedrichsbrücke, jetzt Theodor-Heuss-Brücke, Blick auf Neuenheim

Mit der 1877 erbauten Friedrichsbrücke wird Neuenheim enger mit Heidelberg verbunden. Die Eingemeindung 1891 gibt der Entwicklung des Ortes einen entscheidenden Schub. Ausgehend vom Dorfkern entwickelt sich um 1900 ein Stadterweiterungsgebiet in westlicher Richtung, das vor allem von Villen- und Mietwohnungsbauten geprägt ist.

Auch heute übernehmen die (1964 umbenannte) Theodor-Heuss-Brücke und die Brückenstraße die Rolle der Hauptverkehrsverbindung. Die gut erhaltenen Villenbauten im Stadtteil und Geschäftshäuser in der Brückenstraße unterstreichen den Ruf des Stadtteils als gehobenes Wohnviertel.

The Friedrichsbrücke, built in 1877, connects Neuenheim more closely to Heidelberg. The incorporation in 1891 results in a decisive push for the place. Starting out from the centre of the village, there develops an area of the city´s extension to the West at about 1900, which is most of all characterized by villas and tenements.

Still today, the Theodor-Heuss-Brücke (renamed in 1964) and the Brückenstraße function as the main traffic connection. The well preserved villa buildings in the district and the business buildings in the Brückenstraße emphasize the district´s reputation of being a better neighbourhood.

The Friedrichsbrücke, now Theodor-Heuss-Brücke, view at Neuenheim

Das Neckarvorland

Das Neckarvorland an der Neuenheimer Seite in einer Aufnahme von 1912. Zu diesem Zeitpunkt säumen bereits etliche prachtvolle Villen die Uferstraße, auf deren anderer Seite zum Wasser hin lange Zeit das zu transportierende Material der Flößer zwischengelagert werden darf.

Bei den Häusern entlang der Neuenheimer Straße handelt es sich nach wie vor um eine gute Wohngegend. Zwar hat der Verkehr zugenommen, aber die einst gewerblich genutzten Wiesen und der Neckar quasi vor der Haustür machen das Wohnen in dieser Gegend unverändert attraktiv.

The Neckarvorland on the Neuenheim banks on a photography from 1912. Already at this time there are several splendid villas along the Uferstraße, at whose opposite side the rafters are allowed for a long time to place the material they transport.

Still the houses along the Neuenheimer Straße are a well-respected neighbourhood. Indeed traffic has increased, but the meadows which were once used for trade and the Neckar being so to speak right at the door still make living in this area attractive.

The Neckarvorland (Neckar Foreshore)

Das Schulhaus der heutigen Stauffenbergschule in der Richard-Drach-Straße wird 1926 eingeweiht. Das Schulhaus ist die Bestätigung, dass der Pfaffengrund endgültig als eigenständiger Stadtteil angesehen wurde. Die Siedlung ist aufgrund der wachsenden Wohnungsnot nach 1918 gleichsam am Reißbrett entstanden. Die Bebauung steht im Zeichen der Gartenstadtbewegung und bevorzugt den Flachbau mit Gartenland. 1926 leben bereits 1.900 Menschen in dem weiter wachsenden Wohngebiet.
Die Einwohnerzahl des Pfaffengrunds ist auf nahezu 10.000 angewachsen, folgerichtig hat der Bau 1956 zusätzliche Schulräume erhalten. Heute konzentriert sich die Stauffenbergschule auf die Förderung insbesondere sprachbehinderter Kinder.

Pfaffengrund

The school building of today´s Stauffenbergschule is officially opened in 1926. The school building confirms that now the Pfaffengrund is considered an independent district. Due to increasing need of accomodation, this settlement developed after 1918, so to speak planned on the drawing board. The building of the area is influenced by the Gartenstadt movement and prefers low buildings with gardens. Already in 1926 there live 1,900 people in the still growing residential area.
Today the number of residents of the Pfaffengrund has grown to almost 10,000, consequently the building was provided with additional space for more classes. Today the Stauffenbergschule focuses on supporting most of all children with language disorders.

Pfaffengrund

Blick vom Rohrbacher Rathaus in die Rathausstraße aus Anlass der Einholung der Kirchenglocken für die Melanchthonkirche, um 1925. Feierlich und erwartungsvoll schauen die Teilnehmer des Festzugs in die Kamera des Photographen. Der alte Dorfcharakter mit eingeschossiger Hausbebauung deutet auf die ehemals ländliche Struktur des 1927 eingemeindeten Vororts hin. Rechts ist die 1938 zerstörte Synagoge zu sehen. Im Hintergrund erhebt sich der Turm der katholischen Kirche.

Durch die Zerstörung der Synagoge und den Abriss des Kirchturms 1966 wandelt sich die Sicht in die Rathausstraße. Seit 1985 bildet der neu gestaltete Rathausplatz einen neuen Mittelpunkt des Stadtteils Rohrbach. An die einstige Synagoge erinnert ein Gedenkstein.

View from Rohrbach´s town hall towards the Rathausstraße on the occasion of taking the church-bells to the Melanchthonkirche, at about 1925. Solemnly and full of expectation the participants in the procession look at the camera. The atmosphere of an old village refers to the formerly rural structure of this suburb which was incorporated in 1927. To the right the synagogue can be seen, which was destroyed in 1938. In the background there rises the steeple of the Catholic church.

Due to the destruction of the synagogue and the steeple being torn down in 1966, the view towards the Rathaus is changed. Since 1985 the newly designed Rathausplatz has been a new centre of the district of Rohrbach. A memorial stone reminds to the former synagogue.

Rohrbach

Schlierbach

Romantischer Blick von Ziegelhäuser Seite auf Schlierbach. Der Ortsteil wird charakterisiert durch seine schmale und lange Ausdehnung entlang des Neckars. Bestimmend für das Landschaftsbild ist die Nähe zum Fluss wie auch zum Stadtwald. Bis zur Errichtung der Neckarbrücke zwischen Ziegelhausen und Schlierbach 1914 bestimmten Fährleute das Bild – wie hier auf Höhe des Restaurants Jägerhaus. Rechts ist die katholische St.-Laurentius-Kirche zu erkennen.

Ähnlich idyllisch und beschaulich ist der Neckar in Schlierbach noch heute. Die Bebauung ist dichter geworden und unterstreicht Schlierbachs Charakter als attraktiver Wohnstadtteil in grüner Umgebung.

Romantic view at Schlierbach from the direction of Ziegelhausen. The district is characterized by stretching long and narrowly along the Neckar. Typical for the atmosphere of the landscape is its closeness both to the river and to the Stadtwald. Until the Neckar bridge between Ziegelhausen and Schlierbach had been built, ferrymen were a typical sight – as here near the Jägerhaus restaurant. To the right the Catholic chapel of St. Laurentius (St. Laurence) can be recognized.

At Schlierbach the Neckar is still today similarly idyllic and quiet. Development has become denser and emphasizes Schlierbach´s nature of being an attractive residential district within a green environment.

Blick von Ziegelhäuser Seite auf die Schlierbacher Landstraße in Richtung Altstadt. Nicht weit vom Karlstor liegt der Hausacker, an dem einst eine Reihe einfacher Fischerhäuschen standen; bis 1896 ebenso eine Wirtschaft und das Gebäude des bekannten Feuerspritzenfabrikanten Carl Metz, der an dieser Stelle auch ein Museum für Waffen, Rüstungen, Münzen etc. einrichtet.

Doch müssen alle diese Gebäude im Zuge der Verkehrserschließung des Neckartals weichen. Die Enge des Talgrunds erschwert eine zufriedenstellende Verkehrserschließung, denn Eisenbahn, Straßenbahn und Autostraße stehen in unmittelbarer Konkurrenz zueinander. Auch nach Entfernung der Straßenbahngleise besteht weiter ein enger Kontakt der hier befindlichen Häuser mit der Eisenbahn und dem Kraftfahrzeugverkehr der Schlierbacher Landstraße, die starken Quell- und Fernverkehr zu bewältigen hat.

View from Ziegelhausen at the Schlierbacher Landstraße towards the old part of the city. Not far away from the Karlstor there is the Hausacker, where once there was a number of small, simple fishermen´s houses, until 1896 also a pub and the building of the famous producer of fire hoses, Carl Metz, who at this place built also a museum for arms, armour, coins, aso.

However, all these buildings must make way for the Neckar valley being opened up for traffic. The narrowness of the valley makes it difficult to establish a satisfying traffic connection, for railroad, tram, and road are in direct competition to each other. Even after the tram tracks have been taken away, there here existing houses are in close contact to the railroad and the car traffic on the Schlierbacher Landstraße which must cope with heavy local and far-distance traffic.

Blick vom Gaisberg auf das große Baggerloch, das 1908–14 in Vorarbeit für den neuen Heidelberger Hauptbahnhof für etwas mehr als 15 Millionen Goldmark entsteht. Zwei Weltkriege verzögern die Verlegung und Fertigstellung des Hauptbahnhofs bis 1955.

Baggerloch Weststadt

Nur die Begrenzungsmauer am linken unteren Bildrand lässt erahnen, dass die zwei Bilder vom selben Standort aus aufgenommen sind. Von der Natur vereinnahmt, lässt sich die ursprüngliche Aussicht fast nicht mehr vergleichen, vor allem das große Baggerloch ist, obwohl längst überbaut, nicht mehr auszumachen.

View from the Gaisberg at the huge quarry hole which developes from 1908 to 1914 in the course of the preparatory work for Heidelberg´s new main station which costs 14 million Goldmarks. Two world wars delay the moving and completion of the main station until 1955.

Only the bordering wall in the lower left part of the picture gives the idea that the two shots were taken from the same place. Taken over by nature, the original view can hardly be compared, most of all the huge quarry hole, although it has long since been built over, cannot be recognized anymore.

Baggerloch Weststadt
(Weststadt Quarry Hole)

Christuskirche

Mit dem starken Bevölkerungszuwachs in den badischen Städten seit 1870 geht ein steigender Bedarf an Wohnraum einher. Mit der Weststadt wird die Stadterweiterung Heidelbergs unmittelbar südwestlich der Altstadt in Angriff genommen. Die Straßenzüge werden im Rechteckschema angeordnet. Villenartige Landhäuser prägen weithin die Bauweise der Weststadt. Es entsteht hochwertige Wohnarchitektur. Die Ansicht zeigt den Blick in die Zähringerstraße mit der 1902–03 errichteten Christuskirche.

Hätten nicht moderne Kraftfahrzeuge in der Zähringerstraße Einzug gehalten, man könnte heute noch glauben, sich in der Zeit um 1900 zu befinden. Der reiche Bestand an Kulturdenkmalen, begrünten Innenhöfen und Vorgärten weisen die Weststadt im Kernbereich als besonders attraktives Wohnumfeld aus.

Coming along with a strong increase of the population in the towns and cities of Baden after 1870, there is increasing need of accomodation. With the Weststadt the extension of Heidelberg immediately southwest of the old part ist started. The streets are rectangularly organized. Villa-like country houses are by far typical of the way in which the Weststadt is built. There develops a high-quality residential architectur. This view goes towards the Zähringerstraße with the Christuskirche which was erected in 1902–03.

If no modern cars had found their way to the Zähringerstraße, one might think to still be in the time at about 1900. The rich stock of cultural memorials, green inner courtyards, and front gardens give evidence to the Weststadt being an attractive residential area.

Christuskirche (Christ Church)

Blick in die Mannheimer Straße in Wieblingen. Das Ortsbild wird durch die angesiedelten Land- und Weidewirtschaftsbetriebe geprägt, bis die ersten Fabrikbetriebe gegen Ende des 19. Jahrhunderts zur Ausdehnung Wieblingens nach Westen und nach Heidelberg hin führen. Weiter hinten im Bild der Turm der 1905 errichteten evangelischen Kreuzkirche.

Stark verändert zeigt sich das Aussehen der Mannheimer Straße in Wieblingen heute. Lediglich die Kirche und die direkt angrenzenden Gebäude liefern noch einen Anhaltspunkt für den Standpunkt des Photographen. 2003 wurde die Neugestaltung der Mannheimer Straße abgeschlossen und Wieblingen durch den Bau einer Umgehungsstraße wesentlich vom Durchgangsverkehr entlastet.

View at the Mannheimer Straße at Wieblingen. The image of the place is characterized by agricultural and cattle trade which has settled down here until at the end of the 19th century the first factories result in Wieblingen being extended towards the West and Heidelberg. Further to the background there is the steeple of the Protestant Christ Church which was erected in 1905.

Today the view of the Mannheimer Straße at Wieblingen has changed much. Only the church and the buildings in its immediate environment give us an idea of from where the photography was taken. In 2003 the renovation of the Mannheimer Straße was completed and a bypass decisively relieved Wieblingen from traffic.

Ziegelhausen

Ziegelhausen mit seiner 1914 eingeweihten Neckarbrücke. Der Photograph hat seinen Standpunkt im stillgelegten Steinbruch gewählt und blickt auf ein Dorf, in dem die Neckarwiesen bereits nur noch selten zum Bleichen genutzt werden.
Deutlich intensiver bebaut bietet sich dieselbe Ansicht heute dem Betrachter dar. Die Straße entlang dem Neckar hat sich inzwischen zu einer bedeutenden Verkehrsader entwickelt. Die historische Ziegelhäuser Neckarbrücke (1945 gesprengt) ist seit 1954 durch einen Neubau ersetzt. Die herrliche Lage des 1975 eingemeindeten Stadtteils im Neckartal, insbesondere auch die Fülle der Ausflugsmöglichkeiten in den nahen Odenwald, ein dichtes Hotel- und Gastronomieangebot, das nahe gelegene Kloster Neuburg, ebenso das Textilmuseum mit seinen Wechselausstellungen sowie die Nähe zu Heidelbergs Altstadt und zum Schloss machen es zu einem gesuchten Ausflugs- und Erholungsziel.

Ziegelhausen with its Neckar bridge which was officially opened in 1914. The photographer has chosen his place at the abandoned quarry and looks down to a village where already the Neckar meadows are only seldomly used for bleaching anymore.
These days the same view presents itself to the observer in a much more developed state. Meanwhile the road along the Neckar has developed to being an important arterial road. Since 1954 the historic bridge over the Neckar at Ziegelhausen (blown up in 1945) has been replaced by a new construction. This district´s beautiful location in the Neckar valley, which was incorporated in 1975, and also particularly the possibilities for outings to the nearby Odenwald, a dense offer of hotels and catering trade, the nearby Neuburg monastery, just as the fabrics museum with its changing exhibitions as well as its closeness to Heidelberg´s old part and the castle make the place a much demanded destination for recreation and outings.

Ziegelhausen

Die Heidelberger Bezirkssparkasse am Wredeplatz 2, Aufnahme von 1927. Fast hundert Jahre sind seit Gründung der Heidelberger Sparkasse vergangen, als diese im November 1927 das von Franz Sales Kuhn in barockem Habitus erbaute, „mustergültige" Verwaltungsgebäude bezieht. Die großen Wohn- und Geschäftshäuser am heutigen Friedrich-Ebert-Platz vermitteln großstädtisches Flair.

Die heutige Hauptfiliale in der Kurfürstenanlage, im Dezember 1960 eröffnet, ist zeitgenössischen Zeitungsberichten zufolge „ein erfreuliches Beispiel neuzeitlicher Baugesinnung und damit eine weitere Sehenswürdigkeit Heidelbergs", der Baustil ebenso Ausdruck seiner Zeit wie das Anwesen am Friedrich-Ebert-Platz, in dem sich heute das Institut für Deutsches und Europäisches Gesellschafts- und Wirtschaftsrecht der Heidelberger Universität befindet.

The Heidelberger Bezirkssparkasse at Wredeplatz 2, photography from 1927. Almost 100 years have passed since the Heidelberger Bezirkssparkasse was founded, when in November, 1927, it moves into the "perfect" administration building which had been erected in baroque style by Franz Sales Kuhn. The big residential and business buildings at today´s Friedrich-Ebert-Platz provide an air of big cities. According to contemporary newspaper reports, today´s main branch at the Kurfürstenanlage, opened in December, 1960, is "a pleasant example of a modern building attitude and thus another attraction of Heidelberg", the building style an expression of its time, just as the one at the Friedrich-Ebert-Platz where today there is the Institute of German and European Social and Economic Law of the University of Heidelberg.

Heidelberger Bezirkssparkasse (District Savings Bank)

In der Schiffgasse 11 befindet sich ursprünglich das „Schwarze Schiff“, eine Schifferherberge. Erst beim Feldzug der Franzosen, dann bei einem Brand 1689 wird die Herberge zerstört. Das heutige Gebäude geht auf das Jahr 1698 zurück.
Es war nicht immer allein Gasthaus. Im Lauf der Zeit werden die Räumlichkeiten von der Brauerei „Zum Schwarzen Schiff“, von einer mechanischen Fabrik sowie von den Heidelberger Bäckermeistern als Innungshaus genutzt. Äußerlich relativ unverändert, zeigt sich heute darin die „Backmulde“ ihren Gästen: In der Gaststube erwartet die Besucher gepflegte badische und internationale Küche, das Hotel bietet moderne Zimmer in historischem Ambiente.

Schiffgasse

At Schiffgasse 11 there was originally the "Schwarze Schiff (Black Ship)", a hostel for river sailors. At first during a French campaign, then by a fire the hostel is destroyed. The current building dates back to the year 1698. It has not always been only a guesthouse. In the course of time the accomodations are used by the brewery "Zum Schwarzen Schiff", by a mechanics factory, as well as by Heidelberg´s master bakers as their guildhouse. Comparably unchanged from the outside, inside the "Backmulde (Baking Trough)" presents itself to its guests: in the lounge visitors may expect good Baden regional and international cooking, the hotel offers modern rooms with an historic atmosphere.

Schiffgasse

Neckarvorland an der Neuenheimer Landstraße

Das oberhalb der Theodor-Heuss-Brücke gelegene Terrain wird in den 1870er Jahren zwischen Leinpfad und Uferstraße aufgeschüttet und dient als öffentlicher Warenumschlagplatz (Photo um 1910). An der so genannten Lauer legen Schiffe an, die Waren werden gegen Gebühren gelagert. Flößer landen zusammengebundene Baumstämme an, die als Brennholz weiterverkauft werden.

Heute ist das Neckarvorland Naherholungsgelände, beliebte Flaniermeile und Ausgangspunkt für Fahrten mit dem Tretboot auf dem Neckar.

In the 1870s the terrain above the Theodor-Heuss-Brücke is raised and serves as a public place of trading goods (Photo taken around 1910). Ships berth at the so called "Lauer", goods are stored for a fee, rafters bring logs which are tied together and are sold as fire-wood. Today the Neckarvorland is an area of nearby recreation, a popular strolling area, and starting point for pedal boat trips across the Neckar.

Neckarvorland at the Neuenheimer Landstraße

Über die Autoren

David Depenau

Geboren 1970 in Karlsruhe. Wächst in Karlsbad-Langensteinbach auf und besucht dort das Gymnasium. Schon in früher Jugend reges Interesse an Literatur, historischer Lektüre und Erzählungen der Großeltern. 1989 bis 1992 Ausbildung zum Restaurantfachmann im Hotel-Restaurant Erbprinz in Ettlingen. Nach verschiedenen Berufsstationen im In- und Ausland Besuch der Hotelfachschule Heidelberg in den Jahren 1998–2000. David Depenau ist Geschäftsführender Direktor des Hotels „Die Sonne Frankenberg".
Er ist Mitglied der Stadtgeschichtlichen Kommission der Stadt Ettlingen und unter anderem im Landesvorstand der Badischen Heimat aktiv.

Ernot Drücke

Ernot Drücke, geboren 1940 in Ettlingen. Nach Besuch des dortigen Realgymnasiums Ausbildung zum Photographen im elterlichen Betrieb, der seit 1878 in Ettlingen bestand. 1959 Gesellenprüfung und 1965 Meisterprüfung im Photographenhandwerk. 1967 Übernahme des elterlichen Betriebes in der Thiebautstraße in Ettlingen, den er bis 1999 mit seinem Bruder führte. 1980 bis 1986 und 1989 bis 1992 Obermeister der Photographeninnung Karlsruhe. Seit 1999 spezialisiert auf Industrie- und Werbephotographie.

The authors

David Depenau

Born in Karlsruhe in 1970. Grows up in Karlsbad-Langensteinbach and attends grammar school there. Already in his earliest youth he is interested in literature, historic reading, and his grandparents´ stories. 1989–92 vocational training as a restaurant expert at the "Erbprinz" hotel and restaurant. After many professional stations both in Germany and abroad he attends the school of hotel management in Heidelberg from 1998–2000. David Depenau is the managing director of the hotel "Die Sonne Frankenberg". He is a member of the Commission on Municipal History of the City of Ettlingen and a. o. an active member of the State Board of Badische Heimat.

Ernot Drücke

Born in 1940 in Ettlingen. After having attented grammar school there he was trained as a photographer at his parents´ photographic establishment which had been existing in Ettlingen since 1878. In 1959 examination to complete his apprenticeship, and in 1965 the examination for being a master photographer. In 1967 he took over his parents´ trade at the Thiebautstraße in Ettlingen, which he headed together with his brother until 1999. 1980–86 and 1989–92 he was the First Master of the Photographers´ Guild of Karlsruhe. Since 1999 he has specialized in industrial and advertizement photography.

Bildnachweis

Sämtliche neuen Photographien: Ernot Drücke, Ettlingen. Historische Photographien: Stadtarchiv Heidelberg.

Picture copyrights

All current photographies. Ernot Drücke, Ettlingen. Historic photographies: Stadtarchiv Heidelberg

Dank

Der Dank der Autoren gilt insbesondere folgenden Personen, ohne deren Mithilfe das vorliegende Buch nicht hätte erarbeitet werden können:
Meinen Kindern Neele, Jasper und Mattis für die Bereitschaft, den Papa ohne zu murren zusätzlich zur Arbeit zu entbehren.
Herrn Dr. Peter Blum, Frau Beate Ellbrück und Herrn Günther Berger vom Stadtarchiv Heidelberg, deren Begleitung der Arbeit von der erweiterten Konzeption bis hin zur finalen Korrektur unverzichtbar war.
Herrn Klaus Bouchetob von der Sparkasse Heidelberg, ohne den die Umsetzung dieser Aufgabe nur schwer denkbar gewesen wäre.
Herrn Erik Pratsch und Frau Petra Mayáns, Heidelberg für alle wertvollen Ideen und Kontakte.
Herrn Bodo Skudlawski, Hamm und Herrn Michael Thompson, E-Greenwich für alle Hilfe.
Herrn Dr. Mirko Wittwar für seine Hilfe bei der englischen Übersetzung.
Danke auch an alle Ungenannten, die durch Öffnung einer Vielzahl von sonst verschlossenen privaten Türen und Fenstern erst etliche der in möglichst identischer Perspektive aufgenommenen aktuellen Fotos ermöglicht haben.

Literaturnachweis

DEPENAU, David: Die Ortsnamen in Heidelberg, Mannheim und dem Rhein-Neckar-Kreis. Von Bloomäulern, Lellebollem und Neckarschleimern. Ubstadt-Weiher 2002.
DEPENAU, David: Karlsruhe einst und heute. Vergleichende Stadtansichten. Ubstadt-Weiher 2006.
EHHALT, Dieter u.a.: Heidelberg, gestern und heute. Heidelberg 2000.
ELLBRÜCK, Beate: Erinnerungen an Alt-Heidelberg. Heidelberg 2001.
ZERFAß, Beate: Heidelberg wie es früher war. Heidelberg 1996.

... sowie diverse Internetseiten.

Thanks

The authors would like to express their particular thanks to the following people without whose help the here presented book would have been impossible to write:
my children Neele, Jasper, and Mattis for accepting without any complaints the absence of their daddy in addition to his worktime.
Dr. Peter Blum, Mrs. Beate Elbrück, and Mr. Günther Berger from the Stadtarchiv Heidelberg, whose accompaniment of our work from the extended concept as far as to the final proof reading was indispensible.
Mr. Klaus Bouchetob from the Sparkasse Heidelberg, without whom this task would have been difficult to do.
Mr. Erik Pratsch and Mrs. Petra Mayáns, Heidelberg, for all their valuable ideas and contacts.
Mr. Bodo Skudlawski, Hamm and Mr. Michael Thompson, E-Greenwich for all their help.
Dr. Mirko Wittwar for his help with the English translation.
Many thanks also to all those not mentioned here, who by opening a number of otherwise locked private doors and windows were those to make many of the current photographies possible, which were supposed to be taken from the identical angle if ever possible.

Literature copyrights

DEPENAU, David: Die Ortsnamen in Heidelberg, Mannheim und dem Rhein-Neckar-Kreis. Von Bloomäulern, Lellebollem und Neckarschleimern. Ubstadt-Weiher 2002.
DEPENAU, David: Karlsruhe einst und heute. Vergleichende Stadtansichten. Ubstadt-Weiher 2006.
EHHALT, Dieter u.a.: Heidelberg, gestern und heute. Heidelberg 2000.
ELLBRÜCK, Beate: Erinnerungen an Alt-Heidelberg. Heidelberg 2001.
ZERFAß, Beate: Heidelberg wie es früher war. Heidelberg 1996.

... as well as various homepages.

Bücher von David Depenau im verlag regionalkultur

David Depenau

Die Necknamen in Stadt und Landkreis Karlsruhe

Von Dohlenaze, Holzlumpe und Milchsäule

In den letzten Jahrhunderten bedachten die Einwohner in Karlsruhe und den umliegenden Dörfern ihre Nachbarn mit Necknamen, die auf besondere Begebenheiten anspielten und die mit der Zeit zu festen Beinamen für diese Orte wurden. Um diesen Brauch vor dem Vergessen zu bewahren, hat David Depenau in sorgfältiger Arbeit alle ihm bekannt gewordenen Necknamen und die zugrunde liegenden Anekdoten hier zusammengetragen.

112 S. mit 76 Abb., fester Einband.
ISBN: 978-3-89735-176-9. € 12,90

David Depenau

Die Ortsnecknamen in Stadt und Landkreis Rastatt und im Stadtkreis Baden-Baden

Von Gelfießler, Käschdeigel und Schdaffelschnatzer

Unsere Vorfahren bedachten die Nachbardörfer und -städte mit mehr oder weniger schmeichelhaften Uznamen. Viele sind mittlerweile in Vergessenheit geraten und erscheinen uns heute fremd. Trotzdem trifft man im Alltag immer wieder auf solche Uznamen und fragt sich, woher diese Namen wohl stammen mögen. Dieses Buch – mit zahlreichen Zeichnungen und manchem Mundartvers liebevoll ergänzt – schafft Abhilfe und klärt in kurzweiliger Weise die Herkunft der Gelfießler, Käschdeigel und Schdaffelschnatzer auf.

96 S. mit 58 Abb., fester Einband.
ISBN: 978-3-89735-247-6. € 12,90

David Depenau

Die Ortsnecknamen in Heidelberg, Mannheim und dem Rhein-Neckar-Kreis

Von Bloomäuler, Lellebollem und Neckarschleimer

In seinem zweiten Band veröffentlicht David Depenau die Necknamen zu Heidelberg, Mannheim und dem Rhein-Neckar-Kreis. Im Gespräch mit Zeitzeugen und aus alten Quellen hat er liebevoll und sorgfältig die Namen zusammengetragen, mit denen sich die Einwohner dieser Städte und Gemeinden gegenseitig bedachten und die mit der Zeit zu festen Beinamen wurden.

128 S. mit 76 Illustr., fester Einband.
ISBN: 978-3-89735-205-6. € 13,90

David Depenau

Die Ettlinger Straßennamen

Beiträge zur Geschichte der Stadt Ettlingen. Bd. 19. Hrsg. von der Stadt Ettlingen.
112 S. mit 55 Abb. und 9 Karten, fester Einband.
ISBN: 978-3-89735-295-7. € 13,90

David Depenau

Der „Erbprinz" in Ettlingen

Geschichte und Geschichten eines Hotels

Beiträge zur Geschichte der Stadt Ettlingen. Bd. 17. Hrsg. von der Stadt Ettlingen. 3. Auflage.

120 S. mit 97 Abb., davon 46 farbig, fester Einband.
ISBN: 978-3-89735-226-1. € 14,90

David Depenau/Ernot Drücke

Karlsruhe einst und heute

Vergleichende Stadtansichten

Das Stadtbild Karlsruhes hat sich in den vergangenen 100 Jahren stark gewandelt. Zwei Weltkriege und Zeiten mangelnden Vergangenheitsbewusstseins haben deutliche Spuren im Erscheinungsbild der ehemaligen Residenzstadt badischer Großherzöge hinterlassen. Die Autoren laden den Leser zu einem Stadtrundgang der besonderen Art ein – der Band führt dem Betrachter bekannte und weniger bekannte Ansichten Karlsruhes vor Augen. Den historischen Aufnahmen aus den Jahren 1905–1910, damals überwiegend photographiert von Wilhelm Kratt, werden aktuelle Bilder gegenübergestellt. Auf diese Weise ist es dem Leser möglich, die mehr oder weniger augenfälligen Veränderungen direkt nachzuvollziehen.

120 S. mit ca. 108 Abb., attrakt. quadrat. Format, fester Einband.
ISBN: 978-3-89735-461-6. € 19,90

Diese Bücher und das komplette Buchprogramm sind im Buchhandel erhältlich oder direkt beim **verlag regionalkultur**
Bahnhofstraße 2 • 76698 Ubstadt-Weiher • Telefon (07251) 36703-0 • Fax 36703-29 • eMail: kontakt@verlag-regionalkultur.de • Internet: www.verlag-regionalkultur.de